Spilled Milk

by Melissa Gressok
illustrated by Jannie Ho

Practice Decodable 31

Mc Graw Hill Education

Bothell, WA • Chicago, IL • Columbus, OH • New York, NY

MHEonline.com

Send all inquiries to:
McGraw-Hill Education
8787 Orion Place
Columbus, OH 43240

ISBN: 978-0-02-136286-8
MHID: 0-02-136286-6

Printed in the United States of America.

7 8 9 CTM 23

Sun filled the den.

"I am hot!" Jeff panted.

Ann plugged in a fan.
It hummed.

The fan hit a glass.
Ann grabbed it.

Ann did not grab it!
Milk spilled.

Milk spilled on Jeff!

"I am not hot!" said Jeff.

Jeff grinned. Ann handed Jeff a rag.